P9-DEZ-545

KIRCHNER PRIVATE CAPITAL GROUP
TRADITIONAL MERCHANT BANKING FOR EARLY & MID-MARKET COMPANIES
ESTABLISHED 1985

How do you know...
if you are an
Entrepreneur?

With Proceeds going to:

Christopher Douglas
Hidden Angel
Foundation

Serving children and adults with developmental disabilities

A charitable 501 (3) (c) Foundation

[k] KIRCHNER PRIVATE CAPITAL GROUP
TRADITIONAL MERCHANT BANKING FOR EARLY & MID-MARKET COMPANIES
ESTABLISHED 1985

Editor	Blair Kirchner
Illustrator	Bob Ostrom
Contributors	W.B. (Bud) Kirchner
	Dr. Patrick McNees
	Cameron Davies
	Lew Turnquist
	Armand Lavoie
	Steve Dauphin
	Gary Robinson

Copyright © 2012 Kirchner Private Capital Group
First Edition
Published in the United States of America

NOTICE AND DISCLIAMER: All rights reserved. No part of
this publication may be reproduced, distributed, or transmitted in
any form or by any means, including photocopying, recording, or
other electronic or mechanical methods, without the prior written
permission of the author, except in the case of brief quotations
embodied in critical reviews and certain other noncommercial uses
permitted by copyright law. For permission requests, write to
Kirchner Private Capital Group.

All content in this publication are the opinions of the
contributors. This publication is only to be considered as
opinions from experiences of our team.

Some of the general ideas for the "one-liners" in this book came
from others and were accumulated by various members of
KPCG over the years. We acknowledge and appreciate those
who might have done or said something that resulted in one of
the "sayings" included in this book. We wish that we could thank
each one of you for your contribution to our experiences,
learning and thoughts.

How do you know... if you are an Entrepreneur?

Kirchner Private Capital Group
P.O. Box 977
Gadsden AL, 35902
Phone 205.313.0784
Fax 954.252.2522
www.kirchnergroup.com

Published by: MIRA Publishing

Who are we and why are we writing this book?

Kirchner Private Capital Group (KPCG) was founded in 1985 and is patterned after the original model for a merchant bank: successful business people coming together to help other businesses prosper. The model also embraces the reality that experience is typically acquired just after you needed it. Thus, our cultural ecosystem at KPCG is one that is premised on the notion that collective wisdom is much more valuable than the sum of discrete experience of individuals.

The KPCG team is comprised of successful seasoned entrepreneurs. The KPCG approach relies on our unique ability to tailor custom solutions for businesses that are at any stage in the life cycle of a business. We now apply our operational, transactional and investment experience to address the unique needs of early- and mid-market companies and their investors. Knowing what makes an entrepreneur is a hallmark of our company and is one of the reasons we have been successful for more than 25 years. We value both the quality and quantity of the long-term relationships with entrepreneurs we have built over the last quarter century.

We hope you enjoy this book and find it both funny and interesting. We also hope you find it a helpful diagnostic guide to determine whether or not you just might be an 'entrepreneur'! *You know you're an entrepreneur if you take business very seriously but you don't take yourself nearly as seriously.*

Where do the proceeds go?

Kirchner Private Capital Group is proud to be one of the supporters of the Christopher Douglas Hidden Angel Foundation (CDHAF), a tax-exempt charity in the United States and Canada. All proceeds from this book will go directly to CDHAF to help fund their programs.

Christopher Douglas Hidden Angel Foundation's (www.cdhaf.org) mission is to enrich the lives, health, and social well-being of people with cognitive, emotional, and physical challenges through the use of Multi Sensory Environments (MSE). The Foundation's focus is on the design, development, and, implementation of Multi Sensory Environments and providing education necessary for fully realizing the potential and benefits of these environments. The Foundation's aim is to enable productivity, inclusion, independence, and self-determination for persons with the aforementioned challenges.

Almost everyone has been touched by someone in their lives who lives with a challenge like Autism, Alzheimer's, developmental disabilities or other conditions that impact an individual's ability to interact with the world around him or her. It is imperative that as a society, we work to improve their lives. This is what CDHAF is doing through the donation of numerous Multi Sensory Environments. These environments have enriched the lives of over 9,000 individuals to date.

Purchasing this book will make a difference in the lives of individuals with special needs by allowing CDHAF to design and donate more Multi Sensory Environments. Again, ALL proceeds will go to the Foundation.

You can also make direct donations by going to http://cdhaf.org/donations/. Thank you for your support.

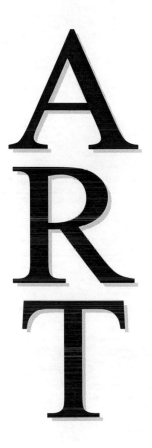

Chapter 1

If you thought about waiting for an
opportunity to knock but decided to kick the
door open instead.

If you are reading this book.

If you appreciate the three most important ingredients to success are people, people and people.

If you are never out of gas or gear.

If two steps forward, one step back is a great day.

If you understand the saying you need to break eggs to make omelets.

If most of your daily calories come from eating humble pie.

If you will take the right apple over a whole orchard any day.

If running your business starts to feel like a religious experience.

If your life makes a Greek-tragedy seem like a soap opera.

If you appreciate it is important to be both lucky and smart.

If you consider Red Bull™ a corporate sponsor.

If as a child you had to explain to your mother and father that the reason they can't find the folding table is you liquidated the assets after your lemonade sale.

If you expect to hit brick walls but do your best to not do it with your head.

If you try to find people to work with you who are smarter than you are and work just as hard.

If you think the notion that everything should be taken in moderation... should be taken in moderation.

If when things are looking better you assume you are missing something.

If you think a partner who agrees with you all the time is unnecessary.

If you are not a hammer only looking for nails
– you are a Swiss Army knife.

If you eat most meals at your desk.

If you consider scotch your current equivalent to mothers' milk.

If your kids report their academic performance quarterly to the family on a grades vs. forecast basis.

If most of the experience you have gained came right after you needed it.

If you occasionally trip over obstacles because your eyes are on the goal... or your Blackberry™.

If you drink coffee with breakfast. And lunch.
And supper.

If when you think of royalty you recall 'Cash is King.'

If your kitchen table also serves as a board room table.

If you find yourself walking the tightrope between reality and dreams with failure in the chasm below.

If you realize the hardest part of every deal is the signature.

If you understand the wisdom in never cornering anything meaner than you.

If you list in your athletic activities 'stretching dollars.'

If your employees have tripped over you more than once when they come in for work in the morning.

If you actually look for pessimists to borrow money from... since they are less likely to expect to get it back.

If you took the road less traveled... and ended up in quicksand.

If your pride and joy will never be able to walk or talk.

If you know to avoid defeat you must continue on after every mistake.

If a 6am call interrupts your lunch.

If you syndicated the sale of your Girl Scout cookies every year.

If you appreciate your culture is the primordial soup from which all things will emanate.

If you never lose patience because you have never had any to lose.

If no drive is complete without a conference call.

If Starbucks™ presents you with the 'friend of the year' award for your patronage.

If neither path at the fork in the road looks
promising but that doesn't stop you.

If you have difficulty thinking outside the box since you never get in one.

If your personal mantra is 'innovation or invention.'

If you know that, as in athletics, prepared average talent can beat unprepared superior talent.

If you have the character to speak the truth and the wisdom to immediately leave.

If you conduct 360°performance reviews with the children on your little league team.

Chapter 2

If you don't worry about bed-head because
you are only concerned about keyboard face.

If you think the most beautiful sound of all is "caa chinng."

If you appreciate that even if you are the only shareholder – there are many stakeholders.

If you acknowledge neither you nor your company will be the same tomorrow, next week, next month or next year.

If being disruptive sounds like a good thing.

If when under tight deadlines you tell your spouse that if he or she doesn't leave you alone, you will find someone who will.

If you know that no business goes according to the original business plan.

If you walk the fine line between confidence and delusion.

If the word 'impossible' is impossible to say.

If determining your true value proposition is like finding the Holy Grail.

If you embrace risk – in its mitigated form.

If you can explain your vision in three sentences and 60 seconds but your mother still doesn't understand it.

If your GPS only shows the road less traveled.

If you spend a large amount of time acting counter-intuitively.

If you realize that no matter what scale you operate at, efficiency is critical.

If you appreciate there is little to be learned from good news.

If you have the wisdom to know the difference between things you can change and those you can't – but choose to ignore it.

If you believe the reason you are wandering through the forest is so you will be first to see the light.

If your mother tried to explain that the church did not necessarily have to be scalable to grow.

If you think what others consider failure is simply finding one more way it will not work.

If you know a business cannot outlive persistent incompetence, but also can't live without persistence.

If you believe Helen Keller was right: security is mainly a superstition and life is either a daring adventure or nothing.

If you actually MADE money in university.

If you learned the first rule of holes first hand:
If you find yourself in one... stop digging.

If you know you have your banker where you want them; having loaned so much money they can't afford to shut you down.

If you understand it takes five to seven contacts with a prospect before they really appreciate the value of what you have.

If you spend less time trying to predict where things will go and more time trying to shape where things will go.

If 'acceptable losses' is an oxymoron.

If you calibrate the speed with which time flies with a 90 day note.

If the right course of action is: Ready, Fire, Aim.

If your leisure time is stressful.

If you know that silver linings invariably have clouds all around them.

If you conclude that with an IQ of 101, on average you are smarter than half the people in the room.

If following a forbearance agreement you start planning your Hail Mary pass.

If when someone says, "That's a good question," you know they don't have a clue what the answer might be.

If you prefer to bite off much more than you can chew.

If CEO only covers one-tenth of your corporate responsibilities.

If you have a talent to use the ordinary and create the extraordinary.

If you avoid paralysis by analysis at all cost.

If you drink your coffee black because you don't have time to add cream or sugar.

If you have empirical evidence supporting your conclusion that being rich is better.

If when cuts are needed you can convince others that you actually are a surgeon.

If 'Liquidity Event' are the two most beautiful words in English language.

If you remember the cell phone number of every one of your clients but not your own.

If the first time you were told you charged too much for your service, you replied that your competitors probably know what their service is worth.

If the stock split in your first business involved your ex and their attorney splitting the stock.

If your institutional investor does not refer to an investor who was subsequently committed to the asylum.

Chapter 3

If you believe the glass is half full even when
the last drop has been poured.

If you live by the Dalai Lama's saying that you measure success by the sacrifices you make.

If you name your daughter Passion and your son Intensity.

If you do not appreciate the humor in a time management seminar that lasts an entire day.

If you find chaos comforting.

If you pray in the spirit of Rousseau – if I can't be better at least let me be different.

If winning is not the most important thing – it is the only thing!

If you think 'risk' is the good kind of four-letter word.

If you find working for someone else equivalent to a stint at Guantanamo Bay.

If you met all the bank's conditions for a business loan, you would no longer need them.

If you expect black swans to appear with great regularity.

If you look at competitors through the end of telescope that makes them look small and the market through the end that makes it look big.

If you feel well-paid until you calculate it on an hourly basis.

If when considering a beer on the flight, you cringe when the flight attendant says, "We do not accept cash."

If you consider your company your youngest child and the only one whose name you can remember.

If you cannot accept that one person can't change the world. "How else does it happen?"

If Occam's Razor guides you.

If the words 'Venture Capital' are bittersweet.

If you understand that when the student is ready the teacher will appear.

If you view mistakes as required stepping-stones to success.

If you understand the wisdom in never wounding your enemy.

If you jump off the cliff figuring you can
create the parachute before hitting the ground.

If you know the only fatal mistake is your last one… and you decide when that one will occur.

If you understand Vince Lombardi's contention that both winning and losing are habits.

If the Sword of Damocles is permanently hanging over you.

If you understand the first rule of sled dog racing; if you are not the lead dog the scenery never changes.

If you understand that rainmaking has nothing to do with the weather.

If you recognize that off-balance sheet financing is the gift that keeps on giving.

If you believe jack-asses were really the result of a corporate project team trying to design horses.

If 'all work and no play' doesn't sound so bad.

If you agree with Churchill that success is going from one failure to another without a loss of enthusiasm.

If you think revenue is sexy and think about it every night before bed.

If your favorite Kōan is — what is the sound of one company succeeding.

If your first incorporation papers are more precious than your birth certificate.

If you thank God for Friday since it is only two more work days until Monday.

If you consider it odd that banks would levy a service charge for "insufficient funds" when you have already empirically demonstrated you have no money.

If free time means taking a washroom break.

If you know what it is like to have two mortgages on one home.

If you have worked so much you refer to your spouse as "The Plaintiff."

If you appreciate the adage from the 'Art of War' that a clever fighter is one who not only wins, but excels in winning with ease.

If your child thinks heaven is a very rich place since angels give you money.

If you keep ending up in the restaurant parking lot after seeing the "EXIT" sign on the way to the restroom.

If your business plan is best seen by a brain scan.

If you consider your children a source of cheap labor.

If you missed you last five wedding anniversaries and it is not because you forgot.

If you take comfort from JRR Tolkien – 'not all those who wander are lost.'

If you equate never making a mistake with never doing anything of consequence.

If you are already planning to purchase "How do you know... if you are an Entrepreneur? II."

Want to contribute a one liner?

Remember becoming an entrepreneur? Have a story to tell? We welcome you to submit your witty and insightful ideas for 'How do you know… if you are an Entrepreneur? II'. Yes, we hope to publish a sequel.

If we include your submission, we will acknowledge you as a contributor. We will not offer any compensation and full rights to the content will be given to KPCG upon submitting content. Send them directly to howdoyouknow@kirchnergroup.com or submit them on our website www.hdykentrepreneur.com or www.howdoyouknowifyouareanentrepreneur.com

Please follow us on Twitter (@kirchnergroup) or/and on LinkedIn. If you wish to discuss this book on twitter we encourage you to use #howdoyouknow and #entrepreneur.

We look forward to hearing from you.